SILENT WARRIOR

SILENT WARRIOR
Finding Voice After Suicide

Kristina Stahl

Edited by Karin Stahl

2016

Praise for Silent Warrior

SILENT WARRIOR is a book of poems by Kristina Stahl that has, with the addition of a final chapter, not one author but several. In the end, all of these caring poets, united by loss, have two things to say: we love, we struggle. The sadness and beauty of these truths inform every page of this collection and move readers to wish Kristina had been able to take the advice she gave herself – take the hand that wants to pull you up.

Debra Spark
Unknown Caller

I have been savoring SILENT WARRIOR. Kristina was stunningly earnest. For a person who kept a secret despair, she radiates and epitomizes openheartedness. She seems to have burned like a surging torch from one end of her life to the other.

Peter Harris
Creative Writing, Colby College

The words are deep, the details are rich and Kristina's insights into how life works are unusual in one so young. As a writer, teacher of writing, and a mother, I know three things for sure: this world is not the same without Kristina's voice, we will miss her forever, and as she wrote, "we are all just passing through."

Pam O'Brien
The Answer to Each is the Same
University of Pittsburgh

This is outstanding. Incredibly moving, heart wrenching, and beautifully written.

Bridie Clark
Snap Decision: Maybe Tonight?

SILENT WARRIOR not only demonstrates Kristina's incredible writing talents but also her complex mind. I read through it in one sitting. But in the end I still have so many questions about her suicide and wonder why, what if, and what now?

Michael Grossman
Investment Officer MFS, friend

The complex spirit and heart of Kristina is so vividly captured in her beautiful writing. As a psychotherapist I hear the voice of many sensitive people who struggle to endure the conflicts of an acutely perceptive intellect and deep soul. Through her words, Kristina's caring for others lives on.

Kerry A. Williamson, APRN
Private Psychotherapy Practice

What a legacy to leave behind. A special, dear, bright, strong and sensitive human emerged as I was absorbing her thoughts. I feel as if I have known her intimately for many years and been privileged to be part of the immediate family, as an invited guest, witnessing her growth and development.

Irene Levin Berman
Norway Wasn't Too Small

CONTENTS

Forward

Kristina Stahl was a young writer and teacher who died by suicide. She had anxiety and was a silent warrior fighting for her mental health. *Silent Warrior: Finding Voice After Suicide*, is a collection of her poems and short prose, along with writings from a few others who knew her well.

Suicide is a violent ending, a complete opposite from Kristina's public face of gentleness, strength, and compassion. Similar to many young people, she wore a mask of achievement and had a compulsion toward perfectionism.

The hardest concept to grasp for those of us left behind, is that sometimes love and mental health care are not enough. Inner pain increases until it's hard to see any other way out. Suicide becomes an option. It's difficult for young people to talk about suicide in our culture of high achievers and athletes. However, there are clues in their actions and words. They often write in their poetry, short stories, journal entries, email messages and social media postings what they do not speak out loud.

Family

Ravenwood Road

it begins here with boiled cabbage
carrots and potatoes
hot corned beef
pulled from the oven, steaming
bridge mix in a tiny bag
with a yellow twist tie
used tea bags in the sink
a red toothbrush in the bathroom
peppermint gum
tissues in the sleeves of her sweater
tiddlywinks
rice in the salt shaker
flower-print skirts
prune juice in the fridge
laundry detergent smells
homemade cookies
the unique smell of fragrance-free lotion
in combination, and all things considered
it was the exact and retrievable scent
of my grandparents' home

A Haiku: To Grandpa with great adoration and admiration

Your eyes give such light
To a darkness you battle within
Your love is what subsides

I found it,
It is safe in my pocket.
If you wish to see it,
Just ask.
I'll show it to you.
You must be very careful.
Hold it delicately,
As though it depended upon you,
And no one else.
How does that feel?
To know something depends on you,
Depends on your life,
Your every breath and every movement.
Does that feeling make you strong?
Does it give you confidence you have never known?
It should.
I take it in my own hands,
And balance it on my palm.
Do you know what it is?
It's very simple really.
Use it to find yourself.
Take what is needed,
What is desired.
Use it as well as you can,
Use it and share it with someone else,
Just as I have shared it with you.
And whatever it may be,
Hold it inside you;
Protect it.
It will become part of you,
Become a part of your thoughts,
And what you say to others.
But do not be selfish with it.
You must put it away for now,
Yet do not hide it.
Hiding it will ruin everything it has helped you become.
When it is opened again, there is sweet music in its release.

Dad's 50th

For the moments that seem to hide
Between the spaces of spread hands
Outstretched, reaching, grabbing for
Something larger, wider
Something heavy
And too great to carry alone.

For your warm heart
And open arms on a weary day...
My tears well up inside
I look up and you hold me still
"I am so proud."
I hear you say.

For the moments you have stood by
In a crowd of people who we have come to know
For your voice
For your smile
Your shouts, cheers, laughter
For your endless support.
You are a steady force
Against my own unsteadiness.

If I fall back you are there,
Grounded.
Ready to push me off again.
I wrote once:
"You pushed me and then I jumped myself,
But your encouragement has never left my side."
That was in 1995.
It's almost time for me to graduate again.
Another year and it will be 1999.
Has time really moved that quickly?

So much of it you have given
So much of your own life you have sacrificed
For me.
For my happiness.
For my life.
For moments like these.
Thank you Daddy.

I look to you and there is
Nothing but your devotion.

I look across that field and I see you,
Your down trench coat hugging the warmth
You fight to hold onto.

I know how lucky I am.
I have so many shared moments,
So many memories I will hold onto.
I cherish your gifts.

My mother, my father, my life –
I cannot ask for more.

Happy 50th Birthday, Dad.
I love you with all of my heart.
Thank you.
Again and again.
Thank you.
You will forever impress me.
Your influence has left a permanent mark.
A permanent mark across my heart.

Mother's Day

A quiet whisper,
A knowing glance,
A calming touch of understanding:
She knows, you think to yourself as you let her pass.

As it always happened, she was there, watching. Like a mother can, she quietly willed me good life, hoping I would see it and move towards where she was, holding happiness in the smooth palm of her hand, holding it out for my reaching eyes. Waiting for me to change, to grow, to learn, to love, she saw it all, silently sometimes. She didn't back off or leave me be, she just was, waiting for me when I needed her, smiling from afar if I didn't.

And years passed such as this, only moments now, stored in thought – flashes of memories and stories and laughter, or arguments fueled by misunderstanding and miscommunication – worn smooth like water over rock, in time. In time.

I once realized in a sudden epiphany of sorts who she was, what she had done, and how long she had been doing it. My whole life, I thought to myself, answering my own realization. She does everything she can, I thought again, communicating my feelings and awareness into some graspable reality. So often these thoughts are forgotten or misplaced or neglected. Perhaps it is still a part of childhood I cling to, a paradox of adolescence, the yearning to let go, to push off and venture, still gripping one's mother's side.

The relationship with one's mother is a curious and hardly predictable thing. How often do young girls question its value at such an age, screaming at the top of their lungs, slamming doors, ignoring her parents, pouting, crying, demanding independence but begging for attention – when does it stop and how long ago did it begin? – a mother must ask herself. Seems like an impossible task to raise such a child. But, one might easily say, without understanding the wealth of its truth, in retrospect, my mother did it, and she did it well. It's hard to completely understand how much a mother truly does for her child, for her daughter, for me. I have trouble balancing the terrible weight of how much I must have constantly burdened my mother, but she took it, always, against the strength of her shoulders, and she carried it willingly.

My mother must have struggled behind the shadows of my father, who, at the times when I remember him most, stood tall, looking down upon the adoring eyes of his Daddy's girl. And there were times when I did not get along with my father, and my mother was there, with open arms, ready for me to fall into them. But I know my mother did double duty sometimes. I know, and this is hard to realize, my mother played the bad parent most of the time, and did the scolding. Maybe it was too hard for my father to do, or he just didn't want to, in fear of losing my love. But my mother sacrificed all that, she gave it up, to teach me lessons I fought to learn. And in the end, years later when I look back on the troubled days with Mom, I think only good thoughts about them, only memories of hugging and smiling through frustrated tears, still lingering after a fight. And I think that is what matters most – the bad days turned into good memories – and it keeps me going, now cherishing the love I have with my mother.

It must have been a moment, or was it a gradual build? When I first re-alized how alike my mother and I were. I must admit it was encouraged by a friend, who, though we are absolutely inseparable now, we were just beginning to be close then, surprisingly knew me more that I knew my-self. I remember the way she said it, as if leading into a really funny joke. She leaned into my face, as if to whisper, but didn't, because it would have been very rude at the dinner table, across from which my parents were seated. I looked at her smirk, but it was better than a smirk, a smile of good thoughts, perhaps, and I watched her eyes tell the story. It was brief, more like a few statements, but it hit me harder than any comment from a friend ever has.

She said to me in one breath, "you are so like your mother, it's scary," and then watched my face for my reaction. A few seconds passed before I answered.

"No," I smiled, laughing in surprise. No one had ever told me that before. "I'm more like my father," I corrected.

"Actually, it's a perfect combination of both," she finished. "You have some things from each of your parents. But right now, I can't seem to make a difference between you and your mother."

"Really?" I questioned, looking again, studying the face I thought I knew. She nodded, sipping her diet coke.

"Uh huh," she added, nodding in my direction. I watched her face as she unraveled a detailed analysis and description.

 "Look at the two of you, your hair color is exactly the same." (We had chosen, each at different times, a rich auburn, which neither of us had ever acknowledged as being similar) "Your laugh is the same, your man-nerisms, what you eat, what you like, how you talk, and even, probably," she quieted on this one, "how you think."

6

She let it settle, watched my face and the thoughts processing inside my head. As if it would be such a bad thing to think like one's mother. I had never given it much thought. We had always been at such opposite ends of the spectrum, I never thought of how close we actually stood.

I studied my mother after that. I mean, really studied her. I watched her every move, wondering how I could have missed it all those years. We were the same. It was an amazing feeling. Suddenly, and it was sudden for me, out of nowhere, I had a mother who understood me (like she didn't know this already), and I trusted her judgment instead of fought it. I was alone in my thoughts, learning for the first time, who my mother was.

And then I began to realize how much I admired my mother, hoping to be more like her, watching how hard she worked, how much time she gave to my father, to please us both, how loving she was to both of us. I saw her in a light I had never seen her in before. It was glorious, inside and out. She hid her inhibitions and I never knew her pain. She was the epitome of woman. Of everything I ever wanted to be.

I am changed now. There are days where everything seems as it should, a predictable schedule, a regular dinner conversation, a TV-side chat. And then there are days when things are different, altered in some ways. Days when my mother and I share intense conversations, filled with detailed stories I can only imagine happening to the woman in front of me, who, as the main character of her adventures, seems more like an experienced traveler than my mom. Though there are certain moments which go unacknowledged in the push of time as days pass, these moments never go unnoticed. I've seen them lately, maybe for the first time, and I am moved, overwhelmed, forever changed. Thank you, Mom. For your love, for your heart, for you, thank you.

A Struggle for Independence Behind the Wall of Insecurity
Autobiography age 13

Ever since I can remember, there has always been the sense of independence within me, yet a need to be near my loved ones and family. Deep down inside the roots of the tree of my life, farther than the trunk, there is great insecurity as well. I am an only child and sometimes I wonder if that ever had an effect on the way I grew up and developed my personality. There is always the need to be around people, especially the ones close to my heart. There are many memories that stand out in my mind like a single bright yellow dandelion in a great meadow of green grass. Most of these memories warm my heart and fill me with joy and laughter...

When I was four years old we went to a resort in the Caribbean. I can remember the pool vividly with its water volleyball net up and the long white bridge that ran over and across the cool watered crystal pool. There was a mini-camp where my parents would leave me for a few hours while they played tennis. I clearly remember running away one day with an older girl. We hid and snuck away, but then she found her boyfriend at the archery range and left me alone. I looked at the pool, at the beach, and finally found my parents at the tennis courts. But I had the feeling inside me when you lose your mother or father in a shopping mall or a supermarket. My heart raced as my intensity rose searching for my mom and dad.

Being an only child, I always wanted to do things by myself, but insecurity and helplessness overpowered my senses at times and left me distraught and confused. Sometimes I blame my parents for having only one child. I had no one to share things with. My mom told me a story once about how a kindergarten teacher called home one day asking if they had ever heard me sing. They told the woman that I sang all the time like a happy lark. The teacher, along with my parents' help, figured out that I could sing perfectly fine but I wouldn't until I knew all the words correctly.

In sixth grade I received the school's Character Award. I was so surprised I was literally shocked. 1990 my travel soccer team, the Renegades, became State champions. In eighth grade this year I was Co-Captain of the girls' soccer and lacrosse teams, although I feel that I don't deserve it. Kingswood Oxford has given me so much and has been a great part of my life. It has given me confidence, support, knowledge, and friendship.

Throughout my life I have accomplished many goals but have also failed as well. I have always been an independent person and wanted things done my way. I am very stubborn. I can never accept failure and in that sense I have always been a perfectionist. Inside I can sense a deep and strong insecurity that swells up inside my mind, ready to explode like an erupting violent volcano scorching the world with its red-hot lava. My emotions are sometimes blocked in my mind, securely locked behind a door, fearing that some day someone may discover my true feelings and run away.

As I sit here writing this autobiography I think about my past and what has been given to me. I think about the future and what is in store for everyone. If just once you could go into the future and find something to bring back to the past, what would it be? I know what I would like to find. I seek true happiness and love in a world where all nations peacefully surround the entire globe. I seek knowledge and success.

It scares me once in a while to think that this is our only life. To think about death is to think about an unsuccessful life, a life where no true happiness can be found, and a place where we don't want to be. I am so thankful for my life; with all my times shared with loved ones and with all the time needed to grow and learn, and hopefully become whatever my mind desires.

Cicadas

The clamorous fire of the cicada call - I wake to its sound in the month of August as if I had known its timing all along. This morning it feels as though I have been waiting for this sound, this sound of what I remember as the heat and high pitch of the summer - the length of haze and heat and sweat - and the summer makes sense to me now. With the cicadas' incessant jarring I know that the summer is both at its height and is that much closer to its end. I am mesmerized by this sound. I hear its hum and buzz and I envy its constancy.

As a child I sat up late one August night with a cousin to watch the cicada hatch from its shell. Sitting comfortably up in my tree with a flashlight, my cousin and I waited, staring down this one particular transparent soul of a cicada. Its shell was so thin and brown, see-through and light like those that were left abandoned, nights earlier, on our lawn. Picking up these crispy shells I saw them as skeletons, little sleeping bags of a molded life. Like my doll house crafted by the hands of my grandfather, this shell was a picture of life to me, both as a place for this creature to live and a figurine to place and put around its world.

But the living cicada was different. True, he had his shell, but it was a little less brown and a little less crispy. A green mush of a thing was inside its worn shell, our precious cicada, buzzing and humming its way through his cage. He looked like he was shaking quiet furies to remove himself from what must have been a tiresome place to live. Trapped. The process was so slow. Knocking hard on walls that will not spread open until the timing is right— fight the timing, call it towards you without knowing when it will let you go. You know nothing of what the world is like outside your tiny world within - you push and push and push without the knowing, the safety or the certainty but only your desire to get there. And you are anywhere but here.

Haunted in this memory I recall the peace and innocence between my cousin and me. It was more than that. I had witnessed a birthing of life. And I wanted it to be mine.

Sports

Silent Warrior

A commitment to a team takes courage. Not the kind of courage it takes to run through the exhaustion or a stomach cramp, or the rain and the blazing heat of the late summer months, though that too is something to be proud of. A commitment to a team takes the courage of a silent warrior, the silent hero who does not work for the award or the win or the cheers from a crowd. The silent warrior battles her self; she challenges herself when no one is looking, when no one thinks she is working. She asks for nothing and assumes everything. She trusts herself and her teammates without doubt. She knows that what effort she gives is what effort others give too. She is not alone but standing on a green field of other warriors, waiting, silently, for the real game to begin.

Coaching

The field is like the classroom; things get done. I seek the potential within a young person, to awaken something within their willing minds. I seek to ignite an athletic passion, to fuel a young person's drive or vision, and to celebrate this connection when it is established.

Coaching is different from competing as a player. I feel at home when I am coaching as the natural extension of the player within me, now learning to step aside and do my playing from the sidelines. It is exhilarating to be a coach and watch my players focus for a game; I feel good about my own contributions in terms of fueling their energies. I am proud of who they are on the field, feeling their wins and losses as if they were my own. I wouldn't trade this experience for anything. My friends who were teammates in college envy my opportunity to continue being involved at a competitive level.

Sometimes I catch myself kneeling and crawling onto the field as I coach; my players tease me but they know how invested I am. They see my heart as I edge closer and closer to the field and it inspires them. They can do what I can't when they are out there. I know that is motivation.

Lacrosse practices were often prepared like a class lesson during lunch with the head coach. It was exciting to get organized and we had a vision for each practice. Game preparation was both stressful and exciting. I am happy with who I am as a coach after my lacrosse experience this spring. I developed confidence and trust in myself. Honesty, expressiveness, and encouragement are three qualities I possess in the classroom as well.

I cherish athletics and the drive to compete physically. It is a strain at times, always a challenge, like a project or paper assigned for class. I put my heart into my job, both academically and athletically.

Thinking about what it means to be on a team

To be part of a team.
To be able to talk to a team.
To know that you belong.
Belong because everyone on a team belongs.
Belong because everyone is a piece.
A piece that makes nothing without other pieces.
Fitting together
Perfectly.
Thinking about what it means to be on a team.
To be part of a team.
To know what it feels like to win.
What it feels like to score.
To defend.
To run faster.
To beat the other girl to the ball.
To be in pain because it hurts so bad to play so good sometimes.
Thinking about what it means to be on a team.
To be part of a team.
To know what it feels like to lose.
What it feels like to get beaten.
It is an ache inside.
It burns.
It burns.
But not for long.
Not for long because the team gets stronger.
Stronger because it learns how to be a better team each game.
The team learns to work harder.
Harder than ever thought possible sometimes.
And this is the best part of a team.
It never stops learning.
It never stops working hard.
It just keeps getting stronger and stronger.
Stronger because it never forgets what it felt like to lose.
Even stronger because it will always remember what it feels like to win.
And there is no end to that.

for the basketball team

It must be something extra today;
something within all of us.
And first it must come separately,
one by one.
And when you find it,
share it with someone,
what you have found within yourself.

It must be something extra today,
something within all of us.
And it will make us stronger
To discover what it means
to learn from each other,
to listen to each other.
and to work with each other.

It must be something extra today,
something within all of us.
And when we put it together
we will have something like a team.
And building a team
becomes the strongest skill
of athletics.
It creates confidence, prowess and
control.

Building a team
creates a certain amount of pride,
a pride that you feel inside.
a pride that pulls at you
and makes you think.
And you think about work.
And you think about pain.

can you feel it?

sometimes I can feel it
breathing down my neck
chasing me
pushing me
telling me to get going
to get somewhere
move somewhere
and do something with my feet
sometimes I feel the burn
and the ache
the sting and the pain
and I think of nothing else
but then I hear you
and you
and you
and another you
I hear everyone
at once
all together, the same
and we are there
this is the moment
can you feel it?
tell me you can
tell me that it matters
that there is something out there
that makes it real
that makes us strong
one by one
separate
together by voice
different places each time
but collectively the same
it makes no difference
who you are
where you're standing
sitting
watching
cheering
playing
it is what you do
it is what you say
how you act
not for yourself
not for your dad

15

your mom
your brother – who else
but for the group
for the team
for us can you feel it?

WHY WE PLAY LACROSSE:

each day is a

new skill a

new move a

better check a

better pass a

better catch a

louder voice an

eager heart a

tougher body a

willing mind and an

endless drive

towards improving

the self

(she wins!)

She is a Runner

She thinks of him when she runs. She only notices this once in a while—his face breaks into her vision, his voice in her thoughts, his words, a funny comment or his touch, his hands at the back of her neck. Her thoughts of him are subconscious and they drive with her as she pushes on. They become part of the run itself. Her legs are in stride with the rhythm of the sound that moves her. She feels faster than she was before. She is a runner now. She knows this and feels it when she moves. She has never been able to run like this.

There is purpose to her running and there is pace. She is going somewhere and she is getting there. When she stops she hardly feels tired and she knows she's done something good. She feels satisfied with her body that day. But there is always the next day and somehow on those days she does not run she feels worthless. Running centers her focus and without it she is distracted, misplaced, confused.

Roads are busy and drivers are careless. Sometimes they do not see her until it is too late and she must run behind them when she gets to a corner because they haven't stopped soon enough at the stop sign to let her pass. She waves if they make an effort to back up, "It's okay," she mouths to them with a smile, "Thanks anyway."

Cars pass her and she can only hear them when they are close. Her music drowns out a lot of the sounds around her. Though it is dangerous she is used to listening beyond her music; she hears cars pass, horns honk, and she looks over her shoulders when she crosses streets. She knows what is going on and she is used to her setting.

There are three different runs that she does each time. Each run is a different distance and covers only part of the same area. In all of the runs, the last part of the run is always the same—the finish. She doesn't really know why and she wonders if she does this on purpose without thinking about it.

Wading Through

My Dream

I remember the day I asked my father whether or not he knew what my dream was. We were talking on the phone. I was sitting in my room at school, it was late in the spring; we were discussing what my plans were for the summer. I said, "Dad, if somebody asked you what I wanted to do with my life, do you think you'd be able to tell them?" and then I added, "Do you know that my dream is to be a writer?"

And then I let it sink in. He was a little quiet at first, nervous to answer. He started with a "Well...," and then I interrupted him. "Do you know that by the time I'm forty I want to be able to call myself a novelist? Do you know that?"

In defense of my father and the wonderful relationship I share with him, I must say I was being difficult with him that day. I hope he can remember that conversation with a smile now, though I know he wasn't feeling so great back then. It was a sensitive moment for him I believe.

There is an incredible pleasure writing stories...when I read a story I truly enjoy, my heartbeat picks up, my thoughts move quickly and I become completely involved with the story, the characters, their actions, and their thoughts. I become part of their lives. This feeling is what I wish for someone when they read my stories and poems.

Folded

Folded into my heart

in neat little sheets of parchment paper that were

thin like a gossamer web

and bombarded and harassed by light night

in sheets of tremor pellets raining down

Help for the helping aid of white lights, sounds and

vociferous clamor

claiming its hold

held still in wrist locks and locking chains

bound into boundlessness

Heave and how its hold

Hells out in shame and self-loathing shimmer

of whitelight nights and blueblack cold and shiver

shouts of terror across the black back bones and spine

ribs across the spine torn and twisted bent over and

back

through a knotted mess of ties and binds

bound back again

out and about its bout of banter

blaze and raze the candor

A height of harrowed hollow lust

Stumped in an empty tree trunk

Her chest of drawers

Moon

You slip over and past me
With your cast
You, my crescent moon,
My everlasting moon,
My shade pulled across the night skyline
You reach me at dawn
I rest

Exposed

Exposed: we part by some wake that pulls you out of me
And takes you back to sea where Poseidon learns your
rapture.
You are a creature of the water: bathed in brine and
bristled with weeds
You come at me strong and scarred and smoothed.
You come at me with your whole being.
You have stories to tell.
When I stare I swim through pages and pages of
adventures on loss and loving and losing still.
Haunted, I rise for more; dauntless, I stroke through
hunger, meeting you at sea.
Am I heedless in my pursuit—this racing toward—

Wading Through

She dreams of a little boy in yellow slipper-feet pajamas whose hair is a mop of wild blonde curls that cover his pale blue eyes. He sneaks up behind her in her sleep and she wonders if he will be hers someday.

He comes to her just when she's close to forgetting she's met him before. She shifts in her sleep to welcome the dream, pulls the thin sheet up like a tent, and lets it crawl in like a curious pet.

The little boy breathes, a calming, heavy stuffed nose kind of breathing; it is the sound of a child's light sickness in the early hours of a rainy morning. She reaches for him but she's learned she must be patient or he'll run away. He is stubborn too.

It is Dusk in her dream, always. The color is the pink the sun makes against pale buildings when it sets—it is warm and soothing but sharp in contrast—vivid against the dark greens and blues of a falling sky.

There is Nature around her in her dream. She is standing on an open porch of a cabin in view of a wide lake that stretches across. This, she figures, is home. Night cicadas begin their incessant chatter in the distant thickness of the coming evening.

Sometimes she sits in a creaky rocking chair and stops rocking to sip green tea from a heavy mug she holds with both of her hands. Occasionally she keeps the tea bag in too long and its taste is thick and metallic in her mouth.

She wishes the light would stay this way forever and wonders why it doesn't. Other moments last longer than this one and she wishes she could do an exchange in her dreams.

His name is Petey and he whispers to her when she's outside on the porch. His voice sends her a chill.

Can I come out?

She only shakes her head. She is busy rocking and watching the water be still. She turns to see his face mushed into the porch screen door.

Can't I?

She waits a moment then turns again to look at him and he is gone, padding off to somewhere else.

She won't see him now for a while. She wonders why she never lets him out.

She rocks back and forth, waits, and sorts her mind like warm laundry just from the dryer. Everything feels soft and there is static cling. She approaches her mind tentatively—she never knows how it'll react.

Though she doesn't always remember when exactly the dream first started. It is like seeing a difference in color. The shades are different, but only slightly. If things feel off, as if balanced on a different scale, she knows she's seen him. Perhaps he comes to her when she's daydreaming at school, rewandering somewhere she's been the night before as she prepares to teach a class.

She's never dreamed of a wedding. Nor has she dreamed of a husband. She's dreamed of past lovers who enter and reenter her dreams like passing through a heavy rain, drenched from the pour. She wakes exhausted, wondering where the rest has gone. Throughout the days that follow these dreams, she is tired and driven by something she cannot identify.

She calls her mother to say hello and refigures out how wonderful she is. She forgets that her mother is an incredible person and it takes her voice of kindness to remind her.

She makes a phone call to her friend during the day. Her friend asks again if she has found a therapist and today she actually says yes. The appointment is for the future and she likes it that way. She doesn't realize how quickly it will come.

Change will come despite the work she puts in to prevent it. She surprises herself when she wishes change. She fears it like a child and only hopes to be dry when she wades through.

She is fascinated with the patterns of the moon, wishing she could wax and wane too. She likes the waning better because of its sound when she says it. Also because it is the act of lessening, and she truly wants to believe that less can be more.

She wants to be alone but she is afraid. She worries that she will not find love again if she lets it go. She believes the return of broken love is the kind that stays forever. She yearns to be distracted beyond her self but can't seem to get through the mess. She is only tidy on the outside.

She is not alone now but knows she should be because she carries the unsaid. It weighs heavy on her hollow chest and she senses the caving in soon. She wonders how others do it and hears from her mother that it's never easy to manage.

In her dreams Petey comes again when she is on the porch. She wonders if there is another woman looking out across the lake just like she is. Perhaps they are the same. Perhaps she has a child too. She wishes she could know her.

There would be comfort in the knowing. She pretends she does and it works. She feels better. She looks out across the lake and speaks to her without words. She knows she understands and imagines what she looks like. She would be so beautiful in real life.

Petey scratches at the screen with his ten tiny fingernails like claws.

Can't I come out?

He is pleading. He is patient, how strange for a child. She wants to say yes. She only shakes her head no.

When can I?

She thinks and wonders without knowing the answer, turns to speak and he is gone. She hears him padding off to somewhere else again and almost calls him back. She does not speak however. She is patient too. How strange it is for her. Perhaps she too is learning.

Another day she is there on the porch when the pink has settled into velvety purple and she watches the reflection set against the dark liquid. She knows she could see her own reflection down there if she went to its edge. Perhaps she should move from her chair but she only does to rewrap the blanket she now brings out with her. It is cooler than it was before. Time has passed.

Funny how dreams mirror the passing of life.

She wills her Petey towards her, senses his presence behind her, and she hears the creak of the screen door and the slipper-feet padding towards her. She is unstartled by the sound. He has come without her asking. She is neither upset nor afraid.

She touches his curly top and fingers a few strands loosely, smelling his baby shampoo. He smells clean but like dirt too—he's been playing out-side after his bath. There is Nature in him and it calls him here. She has nothing to do with it.

Wading through (she's reverting)

I wait to hear something from you
And I wonder
Where it's all going and how's it going to end
And why do I care
And what will I do with myself
After it's been some time
But where do I spend my time
When I can't get any further and I wonder
Why the panic beats me down
Who left who and who will move on
And who will get married and have a child and a family
or a wife or a husband
Or a ring and a home or a law degree or a car or a first
novel and a house on a lake
With the dream the tea the rocking chair and child
I knew his name
I told you that
I knew he'd be mine
I have to wait
Where is he and when's he coming
What will happen and where's the dad or the mom and
who am I
I thought I knew
I never did
Too busy buying things to fill this space
I thought I needed
to fill to learn to understand to hear it from someone
My worth and needs fueled by words like integrity rolled
up into my sleeve
It's so hot in here I can't breathe
We're all just wading through

And When Loves Leave

Your Absence

Your absence is truly nothing
in the grand scheme of Things.

For each new day
in its slight chill and darkness
there is a moment, however brief,
and your absence rethreads itself slowly
on my spinning spool of reawakened thought.
The dull heave that settles under the sheets
finds me as I hide, reluctant to begin my day.
I search for the goodness and the gifts that god gives
me.
In my lack of experience I know nothing of loss.
Do I pray for the strength to let you go and move on
or do I pray for the strength to hold on and be patient
for your return?

your promise

breaks my heart

your slow whisper

comes too late

too long after my tears

but I hurt

and I take you back

without a fight

you don't chase

if you lost me

there would be no search

you say quietly

don't leave me, baby

how can I push you away?

why do you move me so much?

why am I so vulnerable?

I am strong

without you near

but close I am weak

I need you too much

the moon came out so quickly

like waking from a peaceful sleep
that catches you in a moment
perfect bliss--one might say--
there is warm sunlight
poking its sweet hello
through the small square window
more like a tall rectangle
where I see things
like winter and cold
and sunshine dancing
shadows against the ice
that has curled its cool edges
around the trees (what's left of them)
and I sit and stare
I watched the sun set tonight
the moon came out so quickly
rich yellow against
the slate-blue twilight of dusk.
it was so full
I wish you could have seen it with me
it smiled at me and I smiled back

So this is how it feels...

Rest against my chest,
use my body as your pillow.
And take my breath;
use it too.
I do not need it.

Help yourself to my soul,
I've given it to you,
    already.
I welcome your hands
your hands that fall
limp at your sides.

Come hold me,
help me stand up,
Because I am weak when you are near.
I hear your voice
echoing through the quiet silence.
My thoughts are screaming
but I can't speak up

Just listen.

Passing Through

What if I told you that
it's the losing
and the letting
and the going of you
from my life
that I wish to pull back in?

I'd put you back to where you were
or better yet
put you up
front where they
could see you if you wanted
and I'd tell them
who you were.

I'd say you were mine.
tell them you were mine
you were my love
my life my rest
my happiness my heart
my time away from the time
that buries me down.

I'd tell them it was okay
we'd show them
that we love like everyone loves.
I'd let you roll over
when you were sleepy.
sing a quiet prayer for rest
be more patient
let you shower first or
let you sleep in
if you wanted to

I'd doubt less
and love more
take the care to care more
make us strong again
wish you love each day and
each morning and moment
feel the urge to share it
love you all over again
if you'd let me.

How I want it back
wish it back
and will it forwards
to some place
close to now
but I know
there is no chance.

Perhaps

Come find me; tell me you miss my voice
and say that you care
Because I do
and I feel it in my heart
when my hands touch your hands
or merely brush against your skin
I want to hear your breath in my ears
moving, swelling my chest as I rise
    to feel your touch
    your mouth
    again
    Perhaps
    I wait

many years

if there were nothing left to say
nothing left to do
we'd stay here in silence
waiting for something else

you'd tell me to be still
I'd stay quietly sitting
patient
I'd ask you why
you'd nod your head
touch your heart
with the whole of your palm
smiling with your eyes shut

you'd sleep in your chair
I'd read in mine
same old story I'd been working on
without changing or making a mark
time would come for us
turn off the lights
blow out the candles

we'd turn down the bed
pull back the soft sheets
wish each other sweet dreams
night would continue
endless as the beginning of
our silent conversations

we'd love like that
for many years

how hard can it be
to speak the truth
when all there is
is wondering
what it would bring?

chance to speak
leaves the temptation
wet with desire
memory of this sound is clear
fortunate that I may
recall the feeling
like a soft something
in warmth
protection
of a small pocket

You

You make me laugh
when I need it most
   You inspire my heart to feel
when I long for the feeling
   You make me cry
when I pretend I don't need to
   You draw a smile across my face
when a frown has grown instead
   You give me guidance
when my own spirit has lost direction
   You hold my hand
when I need to be touched

And you smile
   Thank you for your heart

the admission

late last night
some strange place I thought I'd dreamed before
sketched its mark in charcoal lines across my back
directions to a future-memory
you're not the only one
who's left me alone
wondering what worth I have beyond this place
I have landed
and feel so strange
so guilty, so wanting,
so needing the connection
between us
flashes of years ahead,
a quick moment now soured in its recognition
now on these keys
I type out this admission (its release is my fear)
what I would never
act out
this yearning desire
wanting for what is not
seems so perfect
I can almost hear words on
the very day
(it's year eight into our friendship)
I'd nod my head and acknowledge it all
and then, though
not at first, but eventually, I'd tell everything
as time would pass, we'd fasten our lives
together like a button to its fabric
held tight in its fit

if

it is the want
I need to give
not the time I think I don't have
if I loved you more
it wouldn't
feel like
such a struggle
to give
a burden
a heap of something oozing
my empty chest
hollow inside
caving in the cave
wishing there were sunlight
to spread around here

help
was there somewhere
but I never asked
so left with regret
painful to be
this stubborn
private
when I tell you

What else

It hurts (not knowing)

What else is there when there's nothing else
What end from a new beginning
I mean the new beginning from such an end
Was that a slip
I thought I knew what I was talking about
How do I manage and where do I go from here

You're still here
Though I thought I'd left you
Where'd we go
When it stopped
No bit no part no life
It's gone without the end
No closure no held glance no if or wonder
What it should've been
What with that what would I do

It hurts.

And when you leave

Who are you to me I want to know
Your face is something
I see me in
Some laugh I've heard before
Some touch I knew it once
Though it wasn't here before
Where have you come from and why now
When I didn't need to find you
You came for yourself
Or did you come at all
How'd you get here
And where's it going
Your skin smells like home
Your hands at my neck
And in my hair
Pulling me back from where I've been
Your eyes I can't let go
And your face
It's captured in my own
I wonder what I've done
And what it means
Or is it nothing—
Tell me this is it something
I thought I didn't need to know
Where'd you come from
And where are you going
If you leave me let me know
I thought I knew what I was doing
I guess I do
But what is this -
Some weird thing I know it's good
What will I learn about me
And learn to give you
Back again if you stay
And when you leave
Will I be a better me
And will I miss you now that I know you
Or do I know you at all
Where's it going and why do I care
You've caught me here and
I laugh because I am happy

Here

Here's the game again:
Wait for him

I remember now what it was like and
what I didn't miss:
the heaving and the thoughts the panic the might and the hope

I should've stayed
You were my safety, my self, my chamber
Misguided and shifting—swaying—catching
Webbed in here it's a mess I've made

I am tangled.

My heart is a rock in my stomach
a bird in my head
a soiled shoe at my feet

instincts

be wary when you see him
be kind and be honest
smile loud and open your arms to
 welcome an embrace
           cry if you have to
 see ... do not weep if it makes you weak
 stay strong and trust your instincts...
            (I trust my instincts and I am ready...no
                    response yet ... I wait ...)

(untitled)

In a minute I will scream. I know this.
But I don't.
There is so much to this silence.
Too precious to break.
Like satin brushing over skin, I remember the taste of your skin
I am haunted by this quietude: this state of being quiet.
I am working on it.
But there is little to say.

forsaken

weaving and threading
    these sorry knots and ties
of love and loss
and wants and acknowledged needs
    and necessary deeds
the Hope rests on a shaky ledge
a little birdie in its half-cracked shell
(protect it)

"when the last word has been spoken,"
forsaken – misspelled of course
forsaken (left as not wanted or
cared for)

Know this

I want you to know that I love
you
and that I feel bound to
you

Know that I am
destined to be near
you
and know
you
forever

Know this:
you
are in my heart and
you
shine brilliantly
through its chambers

Marbles

My heart still makes you up

and dresses you for the occasion of

rememory

and reenactment of us.

The reemergence of us,

the shadow of us,

the mini rememories of us:

the beads, the tokens, the pieces, the candies, the sweets, the pains

and tears

like a jar full of marbles.

With tiny holes washed into it from wear,

I wear your shirt like it's on your skin,

Like I am rewearing you back over me.

Sew it back together.

Remember the stitches

Remember the strings

Remember the things

we used to tie our tiny selves together?

Shadow

My Shadow feels
your light graze -
a memory of you
standing near.

Here I am and here you would be

Retrieving you seems harder now
when these nights are busy with these things.
I am less lucky without you,
less loving, less me.

You've fit inside me nestled for awhile
Like piggies I hear you say.
I feel so alone like I've done something wrong
I feel this guilt—*it's okay*—
I wonder.

When will this burden leave
Stop talking about me - I hear you. I am beautiful
What's wrong with you people
It's now when I wish I knew what I was doing what I meant
to do - what's going to happen *how's it going to end?*

I would like to know you

What is left of today when I wait
for its end
In the midst of its beginning
and why does it feel like wasting
When I am doing nothing
and nothing when I'm doing something
How do you trust yourself
or even know yourself
When there is so much doubt
and you wonder where the time
goes or if there is growth
from the things that you do and the
mistakes that you make

Why want to love and touch someone
when there is so much more you
can do on your own
Why risk the strength you may possess
as an individual for the chance to
feel the rise and swell of love
like a heavy wave in a blue green sea

I would like to know you
A particular part of your hand
or the smell of your skin
I would like to kiss you
I wonder what it would feel like
or if you leaned into me and stared
and made me feel like I was the
only one you did that to

I would like to sleep next to you
or put my arm around you
and learn about your family
brother and your parents

and sit with you
or giggle at some silly thing
and put my face up close to yours
and see myself reflected in your eyes
I would like to care less about myself
when I am next to you
I want to know you by heart
and remember a part of you
that I can recall only with my eyes
shut
I'd like to hear you whisper to me

or pull me close
We are so careful not to get close
though we have sex
It means nothing like what it would
mean and I know you know that too

If we slept together
or touched
or hugged just for a moment
when we didn't need to
would it feel right
I'd like to know

What will you tell me about your trip?
will you tell me you are still in love
with her again?
Will you tell me and tell me all of
the things that distinguish me
from her and make me feel
like I am the right one
but still you say aloud
"but I am in love with her
and I don't know what to do with my
feelings..."

What does that mean when you are with me?
Do you pretend that you love her more
when really you sense something real
when you are next to me?

Do you hear me speak
and wonder if we will be good together?
We will not know until we try.
I am scared too.
I don't want to lose
or get hurt
or hate myself in two years.
I want to learn and grow.

You challenge me
and I know I need that.
Do I challenge you?
I'd be more curious if you said no.
Tell me yes
and I will try too.
I'd be interested in the trying.
This book is complete.
Peace.

On A Mission Teaching

A Mission Statement

I am on a mission and I am being called.
Though I am moving towards a place that is yet to be
determined,
I am at peace with my self and I trust my natural inclinations.
I carry with me certain indistinguishable
talents, strengths, weaknesses and fears:
My devotion to the five senses of sight, hearing, smell, taste
and touch
that create meaning and memory in my life;
willingness to love, embrace and learn;
desire to work and produce;
commitment and loyalty
to those people, beliefs, and things that I care for;
vulnerability and tenacity;
unfailing awe and reverence for life and its mysteries;
willing spirit;
capacity for unearthing experiences;
sudden, inexplicable, and capricious acts of impulse
based on emotional insight; and
slowly dissipating anxieties and insecurities—
Though I will never completely lose you, I can learn to work
with you—
For every day that I forget to remember:
I am always a small sum less than or
plus a little bit more of
the me I already am.

The photograph(er) in kilter

Little bulbs and flashes
snap through panes of snow veiled windows and doors
She cries and holds her smile (in):
Wait!
Hold it there!
And there it is—
Now and known and felt
Maybe one or two or five—
They are where they were still: seated,
hunched—slouched—(disengaged)
heads hanging low (enthralled by something private)
until—one or three or six move and something shifts (the labor):
the engaged mind wrenches the rest of the body up through
Focus, the Redeemer.

(untitled)

what makes us all alike
different
changing
new to our eyes
and ears
and voices of life
and death
and the stones
that tell
the secrets
between Dark walls
and hallways
like alleyways or
muffled streets
with littered floors
speak
or forever hold your
PEACE.

A Tied Circle

"Everything moves in cycles,"
said the history teacher.
"Sooner or later the end will
reach the beginning and it will all be connected."
Is that what's happening
to the old woman
in the nursing home
who cannot keep herself clean
when she eats a meal.
or when the aged gentleman
sitting on the bench
in a park
just stares at a pen on the ground,
that he is unable to reach?
Or is it like the struggling baby
who stumbles and grips to hold
the bottle she's drinking
and the little boy who throws
a tantrum when he can't tie
his own shoe?

At the close of one, so another opens...

Is there time left
    for another Place –
A new space to fill
    and feel
And push and pull
Engage yourself with a
    SMILE
Your wishes do come true

Parent Conference

It's not as though I want them all to know me. But sometimes I wonder what it would be like if they did. A part of me really likes where I am. A part of me really wants to stay. I feel settled here. I feel like I am in the right place. I had a conference with parents and an advisee last night. It was dark, late in the afternoon. The sun had already set thirty minutes before. It feels like winter is close.

I felt refreshed when we met, shook hands, stepped into the adjoining class-room. The big queen chair was left for me. I urged one of them to sit in it: I knew I would not sit in it myself. We played musical chairs until we were settled in. They seemed nice. Quiet, but nice. There was something genuine in their eyes.

A month before, I had spoken with this particular family over the phone a few times. It was the father I had spoken with twice, and I got the feeling he had little interest in meeting me. I felt distanced, cut off, insignificant. Seeing their faces, however, I felt relaxed, comforted by my own misconception of what they were going to be. It felt good to be wrong about my prejudgments. How can you really read somebody over the phone? How can you understand the way a person is going to act if you have only heard their voice and listened to what they've said?

I forgot the power of human contact and the strength and persuasion of an expression on a stranger's face. I realized that though the value of voice and language is important, it was the parents' body language that sold me on my third impression. I liked them very much in person. I was not afraid. We had an excellent conversation. It was candid, honest. I did not lie about who I was or what I had learned from the school as a student here myself. I shared with them as much as I could about certain teachers, their tricks and quirks—it was helpful to have my own experiences. We talked about college, the future, where to begin thinking about all of that stuff.

"You haven't been out of school long, have you?" they asked earnestly. I smiled, shrugged, told them the truth. It was easier than I thought. It's been pretty easy for me to tell the truth about my age. Why hide it when I know it's obvious that I look more like their child than an adult? Why pretend I know ev-erything about being a teacher when in fact I don't. It's my honesty that's get-ting me somewhere right now. My relationships between the families and their children have grown because of my candor. I feel privileged to be where I am at my age. I am not embarrassed about it and in fact it makes me happy. I love what I am doing at this point in my life. I could not ask for a better experience.

So why the self-doubt sometimes? Why the questioning, the worry, the panic late at night—what does that suggest about *me*?

The Mask

You who elude me

You who elude me:
Step into the light from your thin shadow.
Do not be afraid, for it is your self you must fear and you already
live within that chamber.
Your self is a prison, barred with simple cowardice and
misconception.
I am sorry for you that these acts somehow make right of the
wrongs that have been done to you.
Sad that we must attempt to control space (the uncontrollable) to
feel safe in our environment.
I am undaunted: in this heat I steel courage from your stones.

Time

Somewhere along the lines
separating and breaking
the white blankness of a new page,
memories seem to collide and
the truth becomes twisted
and braided with dreams and
realities.

Like the sharp coldness
that catches your breath at the
first taste of winter air, I am
stunned, frozen with my thoughts.

Brought up against the dark
distance of time, I am a
standstill, a landmark,
a timeline against the rush.

The wicked waste of time
is a rush that tastes sour
in my mouth.

How much time
have I passed on, passed by,
walked over, stomped on?

(untitled)

you were there when i thought you weren't when i thought i
couldn't
there were things i never said.
you asked me though you knew i wouldn't say the
always left unsaid
heap of something warm
oozing in my chest so hollow anyway
in the cave it's caving in
bitter as a what'd you say?
can't hear through the
web we tangled in a mess of something else
somebody's careful weaving

(untitled)

not far
not close
somewhere in between
something newer
and greater
that smells
like rain
and talks at dusk
to the sweet
white lilies
floating

Through the pane

The main character is me. I stand at a window pane in pain, watching people carefree, happy and popular walk by. They are confident, and lucky. They walk the tightrope (or go through life) without hesitation or caution. I'm self-conscious, sitting and watching, hiding my shyness. Their smiles never fade, like they're waxed in place. I say "until the fire melts them" because it's as if something goes wrong, melting the wax of a candle standing tall. When they walk on by, and leave my life, I pull the blind of the window to hide the pain of myself, stopping the vision outside and of anyone else looking in at me. I am self-conscious and I become jealous of the carefree people.

change

sometimes I need you to want me
the way I need you
want you
inside my heart, my head, my thoughts
keep tumbling
there is much time to kill
put to death
like a sour argument
that lingers...
tip of my tongue
remind me of my
regrets that keep me mad
make me crazy
trying to forget
the loss created for myself
loneliness is proof of mistakes
am I wrong to ask for changes?
too bad you can't change a person
who needs to change the most
I'm at the top of the list

It's equivocal

Come to my rescue
why can't you?
I'm waiting for you.
He's here but I'm desperate for you
how
do I explain the you
in my life?

Who am I kidding now:
alone and outside myself wondering
where it all began and in which direction
I should go if I have to—
What's with this life we all think is ours to pick apart
Who's there to defend me—
don't make me real when I am gone.
Ask me why and I'll tell you something else—

always there

   it was something always else
or what
   between each (conversation)
there was a tiny little moment
               left for us
or just me
   (because I remember)
to reinvent these scenarios.
               it feels good to do
               this to myself...
               a purging (literally) of
what was
   or wasn't
or was maybe supposed to be

Muse

Come to me (I'm calling)
I'm waiting. Here:
Carefully take this and watch me and
Find me. Here:
Unleash this heavy hand across my chest
There's a rock lodged in my throat and
Pushed down and
Out there and open
Biting truth and bone
Silent furies beat me down
And then your face—
The calm
a quiet echo in my chambered soul
the rue
pores through bittersweet rapture and pain

Alive

Aware
Less frightened than usual
    right at this moment
The music...
welled up though free (all at once)
I am here
Listening
Watching
Waiting
Learning to feel confident
(it is so hard to do)
I am trying
Pieces and pieces rather than the gobbled whole

Climbing the Invention

I make you up through my own perversion
(this sickening dream)
my thickening
and
shameful
shroud
avails me
as
I wait for
the yellowed sun to rise.

A soiled silly shoe on my foot
weighs down on me like a
heavy hand
dropping me into
a deep blue well of waste.
(you never hear my call)

I ...
value honesty and kindness
cherish love and friendship
long for understanding and support
give humor and compassion
am passionate and inconsistent
am working on loyalty
embrace differences but I fear change
I am afraid of change but it happens within me daily
less willing to giving with a risk
less willing to ask
selfish in my needs
I demand more than I return
seek before I understand
push before I am pulled
cannot wait for fear of missing something
am less confident in front of strangers

Each Day ...

I shall listen to my heart as I rise

find joy in something

trust my instincts

be more frugal

improve my ability to adjust to various situations beyond my control

better enjoy various social situations

feel good about myself without someone else's kind words or

encouragement

be less self-conscious

be aware of myself but not too aware that it keeps me from interacting

or listening to others

slow down when I am spiraling—I shall use and believe in my

affirmations

I am no better than anyone else in this world

I appreciate my life.

Leaving Lemon House

She waits to lock the door behind her; setting the alarm is difficult some-times. This is the last time she will do this. She listens for the sound to warn her the house is successfully armed. Like always, she listens carefully, hoping she has done it correctly. She does not look back when she steps down the porch steps to her car. When she drives away from the house she knows she will never step inside its strange rooms again. There is peace with her now, though it is bittersweet, and she feels the feeling everyone has told her would come.

She feels reluctance. But when she turns to smile to her companion sit-ting beside her in the front seat she knows everything will turn out better than she expected. There is time to think about all that has happened. And now she is leaving, driving away to a different place and to a differ-ent city she can call home.

Boston. For now, she hopes she will at least learn her way around the area where she will live for the summer. But she knows it will take a lot longer to learn her way around than that. She does not think about it again for quite some time. She is quiet, and she remembers.

God, she wishes she could be back, for a second, and hear the laughter in the car. Driving towards campus. Graduation morning. Gowns zipped, caps in laps, the music loud. Sun shining, windows down all the way, everyone sipping bottled water to cure a dehydrated body from the night before. She will never forget the combination of sound and smell, the feeling of being in that car, the five of them, going together as if they had been the best of friends all year. She wishes it were true now. She wanted it to be true then. She pretended it was true. And she hoped they were doing the same.

Congratulations on your graduation, a major milestone in your life!

The cards and notes are all the same, all of them thoughtful but over-whelming. There is nothing she can do but say thank you, smile and write a letter to show her thanks. But she wants to show more. She wants everyone to know what she is feeling, how she is having trouble realizing the seriousness, the wonderful weight of all that is happening to her now. She wonders what her friends are feeling too. Do they think about the things she is thinking about? She knows they are all away, home, or traveling, vacationing in some European country. What to do next, she thinks to herself. She has no idea.

Reemergence of Self

You may not remember how it was between us. You may have quieted your heart. But I wonder if your heart has things to say to me. I wonder if your heart is interested in sharing its feelings with me. I know my heart and I listen to its call. There is something going on within it; I am aware of its song and muse. I feel it and hear it speak to me. Do you listen to your heart? Do you hear when it speaks to you? Listen for it. What does it say? Have you learned to ignore it? Have you learned to put it aside from your daily activities? Have you trained your heart to be still? Call to it. See if it hears your call. See if it responds to your call.

This reemergence may take years. But, no matter what, we always re-emerge as the better of our selves. We always come alive again after a fall. We stand up again, and again we fall some time later. We are always tumbling through life—we are gymnasts in this meet of life and body. Our souls the judges, we work and patiently we wait for the verdict, the final score, the points to advance us through our lives. We have no control over the score. We have no control of the other judges' opinions of us—we cannot control what others think of us.

We can control our selves and our hearts. We can control how hard we work and how much effort we put into the presentation. Living is an art and we use and reuse its craft. We are molding our selves to be better and stronger and healthier than we were before. Some people work with us while we are moving and some even show us the way. They may take lead and step in front of us to show us how to act. We may model or mask what they are showing us. We may take what they do quite literally. We may move away from or reinterpret their methods of interacting and moving forward. We may make our own versions of this path—we may stray when we see a patch well worth stepping on. Or, we may ignore their footprints or ignore their kind words and we may diverge from them completely.

We may never find a connection with another person. Our lives may be a series of disconnects. We may never find our selves in the mass and mess of things and people to do and become. We may never see the light or hear the sounds of peace within our souls. We may never listen for the stillness that follows this calm of truly knowing oneself. We may lose chance after chance of opportunities to grow and learn from what not to do.

When we recover from a fall, we may learn its lesson the hard way, for there is no easy way to learn something. Even loving takes work. When it comes naturally we feel it as a blessing, but this natural love is a curse because it does not force us to better our selves or better the person next to us. A natural love leaves us stagnant in a period of stasis. Non-moving non-stepping stasis. Like drowning in quicksand. Oh, the weight of that sand and its pull on our bodies. It's a haunting terror trapping our hearts.

To escape the quicksand, we must be willing to change our perspectives each day. We must be willing to switch our seat in the classroom, choose a new road to take us home, sit in a different spot while eating our lunches, or speak to a new friend each day about something that does not concern our selves. Reach out. Take the hand that wants to pull you up. Grab onto that bar yourself and *pull yourself up*.

Jumping Stars

She sat at her dining room table staring down her computer screen and furiously continued to type and retype, backspace, curse the sticky h, backspace and retype again. It was a bright and sunny Sunday in late July and she was inside her dark and filthy-windowed apartment being ridiculous. She was thinking of too many things at once (a curiously never addressed bad habit) and they were piling up inside her dirty bag of anxiety.

She was trying to focus each one of these many things into one giant beginning of a first novel. She knew it was comical, cliché, pathetic and sorry to dream of her novel before its existence and beyond its very meaning and definition of the word itself. She wanted the dream before the reality, the house before the husband, the love before the loss, work and commitment, the perfection without the practice. She wanted honesty and truth without effort and the strength before developing the source.

She wanted the work she *did* put into things to pay off—she wanted recognition and assessment. She wanted to be good, right, and strong. She wanted to be vocal and clear, expressive and accurate. She wanted to be focused and attentive, driven and dedicated.

She wanted a vision and a passion to fuel her push towards rather than her pull away. She wanted to let go of something and witness its return. She wanted to know before the learning, and to understand before the mistakes and the lessons. She wanted to be before she was.

She was busy jumping stars trying to beat herself across her own sky. *You're wasting it* she hears a voice whisper from within.

And so she tried to listen to it.

The Well Runs Dry

My Soul

Lay me down to rest and
let me rise in peace and happiness.
Let me forget what troubles me
and grant me my own forgiveness
for what I am trying to control.
Let me see the goodness in those
that I suspect of trouble
and indifference.

Grant me the self assurance to
know what is right.
Let my strength in instinct carry me
through this cloud of doubt and fear,
and let me win my soul.

Lay me down to rest and
grant me rise in peace and happiness
Days and nights keep turning;
I as their witness fail to see
their beauty.
Let me see their beauty.

Reach into the well

Wake to find the story wound up
like a wilted napkin in your sweet fingers.
Where is the action, the motion,
the movement toward personal advancement?

Some things never change and yet
this timelessness, this caged moment
of silence under thick and heavy
pressure pushes me under.

I wait, watching, wanting, pulsating
I think, hold it still and quiet.

This thump of the heart, beat of the soul
your enemy is knocking
the self
the giant
the shameful, dauntless self

Take heed
take careful heed.
I am sheltered, scowling, skulking round the bend

Reach into the well with
stones slippery with aging slime
and creatures' excretions
and capture this rage ...

there is no end

my nail scrapes rough against
the cement wall
there is filth underneath
blackened with dirtiness
and there is shame
tender cuticles
bleed with irritation
and I am left with a guilt
again I draw the nails
against the wall
coarser this time
how much hurt can I handle?
my hand shakes
I am nervous with my own temptation
I think about the end
the consequences
I have chewed and bitten upon
the thoughts are old
but they never go away
torn at the edges
so common it is comfortable to me
it is my weakness to accept this
as it is
to take no chances
to change it
I just wait
and that makes no difference
goodnight
there is no end
aggression

stand back

run towards
fight against
the will to die
the strive to live
the drive to be
again we see
the world at most
at one my time
to rest alone
and far beyond
a place for many
but few to go
climb the wind
watch it grow
faster now
your breath is mine

wounds

think
about what
you hate to think about
what you hate to remember
what you can't forget
what makes your skin crawl
what makes the heat rise in your cheeks
what takes your drive
and gives you shame
rips your heart apart
open
the wounds are wide

get the words out

step in time
make the match
coincide with the rest
I am here
moving – stepping – running,
making a mark
to whom it may concern
a sweaty grip on a black fountain pen
the ink swimming from the tip,
rushing to get the words out
on the page
out in the open
threatened to be revealed
I lose them then
gone in a flash
a quick moment for you
for me, hours
of just time
time to waste
throw away
crumple up like the pages I hate but
long to love
wish they were good
my life
like his life
like her life
like all the other lives
goes
unpredictable – unnoticed - unsuspenseful
it just goes
it's inside me somewhere
a fear, I guess
don't leave me alone
listen very quietly
slowly, the desperation of silence
will go away

Resolution

Resolve to describe
      the jolt of winding down
           the steep iron spiral and
                the clank and stomp as
                      things fall on its jagged
      case.

                      The sound of
                falling without
                hitting bottom is
            the losing and the letting go
        of truths, places, things, conversations,
and feelings in your life that you have lost hold of
        your memory.
                Watch this happen.
                    Reverse your position
                      and step outside
to see your self,

                over the railing of
            your form, your figure, the case
        you carry yourself in.
Resolution: nothing is fixed here.

Today

A whispered: *I miss you.*

It lasted. And for a long time I held on to the sound of words
carried through my ears deep into my heart.
Is it there with me now? How can I tell?

Sometimes I can pull it out,
separate it from the other sounds of regular things
and I can feel it touch mine.
There is nothing like this.

Listening to music is the best thing I have done in my office yet.
I feel like me more than I ever have here before.

Yes, you, I feel like you.
Are you really somebody called me?
Answer that.
Slow down.
Are you there yet?
Answer your own questions please.

Writing words writing words writing words
Typing them fast
Keep going something will come out of it
Free write your way through life
Just keep it going like there is something out there

There is something there
please find it
no more periods or punctuation
how about spelling
don't press delete
just keep going
you just did it
you keep doing it
go faster faster faster
let something out what is it?

Keep going
where are you
what do you want
are you listening to me?

Erase

Unresolved

Circles and circles of us pass through separate moments in skipped over memories and sorry conversations that are regretfully incomplete, and together they add up into a series of disconnects in all of our lives.

We all have these memories, a friend reminds me, but even then I sense the thinness in her voice when she speaks over the line. She knows she is wrong even when she is busy convincing me that these certain disconnects don't matter.

The truth is this: if you cannot acknowledge their worth and existence, you never move forward. These moments come back at you at any time on any given day when you least expect them to hit you: it could be a flash of what once was, that is no longer, but seems as real as it was when it first existed. It is a memory of a loss, a recapturing of feeling, a bleak and real reminder of life and suffering in one scene within one's mind.

It is your sensory recall, and it haunts you when you leave things unresolved.

Try this one: don't let something go unfinished if you can spare the energy to work on its closure.

Weeping Willows

The safest place I have ever dreamed of was protected by very large weeping willows, a childhood escape into my own reality created within those tall, droopy trees. When the wind blew, the soft feathery branches of the trees danced in the breeze, and I know I danced with them. A small brook bound the property on the north end, a thin stream really, which dribbled and gurgled over smooth stones. A beaver dam was sometimes object to my young curiosity, and I would circle the pile of twigs, just wondering. I often wondered about those dams, how they served the purpose of home to an animal I knew nothing about. In my childhood madness of imagination I was driven by the desire to play in little forts or villages I would dream up, or sometimes even create with my surrounding props. I call them props, these things:

Happiness: Wrapped in my joy like a Christmas present tied with a gold bow, I am bursting to be opened by a child so filled with excitement it is shattering.

Anger: Could you push me anymore? My skin flares, my heart races and I am running. In fear, in anger, I run to escape it. Denial bottled up in a sea glass 1977 chardonnay.

Frustration: Tear at my eyebrow hairs, pull at my wisdom teeth, tickle me 'til it hurts, then you'll know my frustration. Within it all, you keep spinning. And spinning. My battle with you is never ending.

Love: You are an ache inside me. Share my breath, touch my lips. A secret whisper, silence. A look that tells me everything. I know. And I love you for it.

Sadness: Heartache. Gripping my insides, flushing my thoughts. I've lost focus because of your sadness.

Hatred: Death. Fear of me. I need control. Somebody save me.

Confusion: I don't know what to think. Don't let me carry your confusion too. At least pick up those pieces.

Relax. Forget. Breathe. Just leave me alone sometimes. What would you say to me if I told you everything I was thinking? Would you listen to me? Would you hear what I was saying or would you block it out and only hear my silence?

It's hot in here. Maybe it was a lot of things. But I put myself to bed that night. And I remembered to change the trash bag but forgot to brush my teeth.

Unbearable

Quiet questions within
become snarling doubts
Connecting razor sharp coils of fear
surrounding the soul
Smothering every breath of hope
until no longer able to trust
tomorrow's promise of relief
Weariness trumps the voice of courage
to fight again
And so eyes see only
the peace of surrender
Outmatched in that terrible moment
of unbearable pain

K. A. Williamson

The New Normal

Suicide Kills

Suicide is a decision of impulse,
with permanent consequences.
Suicide kills more than the person;
it kills dreams and hopes for all of us left behind,
the little joys in everyday living.
Suicide tests faith in ourselves.

Suicide brings doubt,
changes our view of the past and future forever.
It means we question all that we thought
to be true and real about the one we loved.

Suicide defies understanding, unravels the mind.
          strains our heart, expanding it with grief,
contracting it with pain.
Suicide kills plans, detracts from purpose,
and challenges our own life mission.

A decision made by one,
an impact forever on others.

Karin Stahl

Something Missing

Two years ago tomorrow she was gone.
Her car which usually arrives by dawn
Was missing from the lot,
A bit suspicious is it not?

It was September 11th 2002,
One year had past
Since the towers stood last.
Of all those who were lost I never knew.

A gloomy day across the nation without a doubt,
But an even darker cloud over my high school stood out.
Though it was a beautiful day,
I felt something missing in a terrible way.

Of course I knew she was gone,
But didn't want to say it praying I was wrong.
If I spoke the words I would be crossing a line,
That would send a chill down the spine
Of a small community.

I kept thinking to myself maybe she is just sick,
Or perhaps it was some kind of trick.
Although this joke would not be kind,
It was an excuse to keep her death out of my mind.

I still can't believe I made it through that day
Without reflecting on the lives that were taken away.
Even at a service in honor of those souls
I couldn't stop thinking of what happened to her
I needed to know.

Why couldn't my teachers look me in the face?
Did they not think I noticed something wrong in this place?
They knew what I knew but they didn't tell
Did they think they could protect me from one less day in hell?

What they didn't know is that I was picturing her funeral in my head.
I poured my soul out to her friends and family,
Telling them what an amazing teacher, coach, and friend she had been.

Finally, the phone rang and my friend confirmed what I already knew
she had died that morning it was true.
All I could do was cry.
My coach, my best friend was gone,
And there was nothing to be done
There wasn't even a goodbye.

Or was there?
Is that what she was trying to say,
The night before when, in tears, she walked away.
Did she already know?
Had she made up her mind?

Two years later I still try to understand.
However, I know that will never be possible.
Some people tell me it was her time; she had no more to give
But I don't accept that
I know she yearned to live.

I know it's not my fault, but it's hard not to think
how I was mad at her over something so insignificant.

I just hope she knows I'm sorry.

Laura Williamson

Aftermath

left are the photos
on stands
in frames
in books
collages of her life fill the house

left are the words
poems
papers
journals
her address book
a last grocery list matters now

everywhere
gaps
empty spaces left
not just corners, closet shelves
but huge ballrooms, entire dining rooms
deep holes we now have to keep
walking around
sometimes wishing
we could fall in, too

as we stay
circling her absence

she couldn't have known

Pam O'Brien

Life Goes On

life stopped
completely
abruptly
totally
the day she died.

lost sounds, sights, smells, smiles
only child
daughter we loved so much

exercise, work, talk
live as before
then after
move forward
go back

just the cliff we fell off

rescue her
follow her
pull back
understand
consider
won't go there...

so, where does life go on?

Karin Stahl

For Stahlzie

If only you knew the way that you still echo in my life,
how you are alive through the moments of recognition –
how I can drive by Larch and see your silhouette in the hallway,
through the screen, or
as I walk to class, lift my head and glimpse you
laughing on the barn landing.
And I feel enriched by whatever you've brought me,
these moments of connection, amidst the impoverishment
of your absence.
I will carry you with me when
I walk across that stage and grasp that diploma
that is mine that is yours.
It is one small thing I can do for you,
to pick up my teammate, carry you with me
and say we have finally won.

Kara Hooper

You are

You know this now.
           You are of the light
           You are in the light
           You are never alone.
                   Please remember
                           You are love
                           You are loved
                           You are loveable.

                                   Laura Spinella

A Sestina Before Dying

In all my life
I've never seen such beauty
Or such life
In the final moments of death
Finally God I did not hate
And I knew what they meant by release

Letting go is foreign, but your hand I did release
But not before the draining vigor of life
For so long I was filled with such hate
When I should have been savoring the beauty
Because I know I am not hurt by death
But instead by love

What does it mean to love
Now I know, it is the ability to release
Someone else to death
While going on with your own life
Stuck with the memory of their beauty
And nowhere to direct anger that feels like hate

Some say that love is the opposite of hate
Without one the other doesn't exist, no love
I find that hard to believe when I think of the beauty
In moving on, forgiveness, compassion, and release
We unveil another falsehood that it is not life
That is the opposite of death

Birth is of course the opposite of death
Well they, you, ask what of hate
Not respecting the value of a life
Is when you haven't experienced love
So anger is your only release
What you've missed is beauty

If you missed beauty
You were like me before her death
To find another person to serve as your release
From a time and place filled with so much death
Is yes, love
You must, lest you deny your right to life

It is not people, or death we hate,
We are angered by love
This indescribable life

Laura Spinella

Broken

I knew of a bird, who thought it couldn't fly,
So it sat in its nest where it felt more at home.
Other birds flew, diving low, darting high,
And this bird knew of safety, though it was alone.

It sang out love songs of beauty and passion,
It knew not a day without wind in its feathers.
It sat thinking quietly of its eyes and their fashion
That kept it from flying like all of the others.

What a beautiful bird, the other would say.
How its colorful feathers must flash in the sun.
When it dips and it flutters on bright clear days.
That bird wouldn't fly like any other one.

All the other birds knew the beauty they saw
In the nested one's coat, and the songs it sang clear.
And as others circled, they gazed down in awe
At the bird with no sight and a heart full of fear.

Though this bird could not see, it had visions of flight,
And the songs that it sang were filled with a knowing.
It knew about soaring and the fact that, when right,
It would fly on its own to find a great loving.

So for many years the bird sang to the air
From the air came replies of birds that would hover
But few would get close; at most they would stare,
They knew of the beauty, but of its feeling, they'd never.

As the time passed on, the bird felt painful longing,
And found in its songs the comfort for such,
But this pain and its comfort they seemed to be wronging
What the bird knew of love, which in times past was much.

So late in one day, with other birds watching,
This singer stopped singing and stood in the nest.
The other birds roosted on limbs they were catching
And the blind bird lit off to fly like the rest.

The blind bird climbed skyward and sang to the trees
It was more than just wind that whipped past its body.
It thought, it is not only a sighted bird that sees,
Blind birds can fly, but they fly when they're ready.

Christopher Weed

shadows in the storm

The turbulence within the storm
causes unsettled structure.
Among the unrecognizable disarray,
how can something true take shape?
The purpose of each distinct gust
Is the destruction of reason, the delineation of all that is
defined.

From chaos, what can be forged?
Within this swirl, what can take hold?
When that which is sound, structured, understood,
becomes indistinguishable,
answers dissolve in the newly blurred vision of hope.
The ascent of descent advances without warning.

This truth lingers,
beyond the glow of the mind's flame.
There, it circles, hovers,
a silent predator lurking under cover of darkness,
outside the realm of consciousness.
Ignorance heightens its effects.
What it desires, it only knows.
From where it approaches, it only goes.

Build the fire, spread the light.
The vibrant colors of life will carry this fight.
Add coals to the base,
Which will expand the perimeter of sight.
Peer in darkness no more –
As dawn replaces the night.

Benjamin Terry

Grave Tending

A soft Autumn breeze
rustles colorful leaves across the grave.

Silk flowers sway bravely,
graceful in the mild November morning.

Leaves flutter down from
sheltering trees.

Birds chirp nearby, assembled for practice flights
before heading south for the winter.

The river is calm now after month-long,
seething, torrential rains.

Geese and ducks paddle softly,
languidly, effortlessly, afloat.

My heart aches as I tidy up the grave.
Nature's beauty helps, but not enough.

I want to dig up her grave, pry open the casket lid,
hold her, keep her safe, make her happy again.

My empty mother's arms and hands
return to pulling weeds.

Karin Stahl

Afterglow

faint light
streaks through clouds
sunset comes
spectacular show of
clear bright light
in her presence
ended
yet we bask still
in sunset memory
sharing the afterglow

Karin Stahl

Voice within

I shall make it a point to recognize my mood
each morning I rise:
positive mood, I shall rejoice in the blessing;
negative mood, I shall focus on its source,
attempt to redirect my anxieties and fears.
I shall meet my anxieties and fears head on:
not dodge issues or make excuses,
remember that each day holds small joys,
even when I am suffering; especially when I am suffering.
I shall exercise sound judgment.
assess myself as accurately as others,
give when I can and consciously feel at peace
with myself when I say no.
I shall not blame myself for saying no to others;
instead, acknowledge my efforts when I say yes,
put effort into living guiltlessly and shamelessly.
I shall forgive myself of my mistakes,
believe in my own worth,
focus and refocus my thoughts when they turn negative.
There is a great deal of love, peace, and strength in me.
I am learning to hear and listen to the still, small voice
within.

Kristina Stahl

Acknowledgements

My husband and I are deeply grateful for so many who have supported us since Kristina's death. Special thanks for those who have made this collection and book possible.

Jennifer Finney Boylan, a former professor of Creative Writing at Colby College taught Kristina and asked us the initiating question, "What are you going to do with Kristina's writing?" She brought professional and personal inspiration as a compassionate guide for the project, as well as being an amazing friend to us.

Kara Marchant Hooper and her father, Geoffrey Marchant, both graduates of the Bread Loaf School of English at Middlebury, labored on the detailed work side-by-side with me to edit and select writing from the treasure Kristina left behind.

Christopher Weed, Kara Schiebel Kacmarcik, and Shannon Tracy Bergquist journeyed each step of the way with love and understanding as Kristina's friends. Rhonda Mitchell, with her exceptional talent, provided the design and editing support to pull us all together.

Thank you.

Kristina Stahl
1977-2002

61471548R00066

Made in the USA
Middletown, DE
11 January 2018